SILENCE & SURVIVAL

Dr. Melba Mota

SILENCE & SURVIVAL

Published by MYJOY Publishing House

ISBN: 979-8-9917191-6-2

Printed in the USA by 48 Hour Books (www.48HrBooks.com)

DEDICATION

To the women who learned how to survive before they learned they were allowed to leave.

TABLE OF CONTENTS

FOREWORD

Some stories are not written to provide an explanation. They are written because through silence work was being produced.

Silence & Survival is one of those books.

This testimony is not an attempt to persuade, impress, or to try the accused. It does not yell or scream to weaponize pain. Instead, it offers something rare and honest: a faithful account of what it looks like when survival in the moment becomes what holds you in reoccurring seasons. This testimony speaks of obedience, becoming the quiet thread that keeps a soul intact.

What you will encounter in the following pages are shaped by restraint. The author tells the truth without punishing anyone on the page. James 3:17 reminds us that "the wisdom from above is first pure, then peaceable, gentle, open to reason." That wisdom governs this narrative.

This book matters because many people do not leave unhealthy situations loudly, but instead they stay and survive faithfully. The chapters of this book name what many have lived but have not verbalized: survival, waiting, obedience as protection, warnings that come in the night, the slow end of survival, and the sacred distinction between chronos and kairos—between time that passes and time in which divine intervention occurs.

Silence & Survival honors the reality that faith does not always shout or engage in war. Sometimes faith watches, and faith waits. Faith endures what is not yet understood all while, trusting that "the Lord is near to the brokenhearted and saves the crushed in spirit" (Psalm 34:18). The author does not pretend that survival is the same as living, nor does she rush the reader toward resolution. Instead, she allows God's timing to remain God's.

This book is a voice that speaks directly to women who wake up years later and realize that what they survived shaped them but did not finish them. There is a particular agonizing feeling that comes when you discover that you must learn how to live again. Scripture calls this kind of rebuilding a work of restoration: "He restores my soul" (Psalm 23:3). Restoration is rarely instant but can be quiet, intentional, and can be costly. This book does not rush that work but walks strategically.

One of the most sacred movements of this story is how it leads the reader to the foot of the cross. The cross here is a place where clarity finally meets surrender, where obedience is no longer about endurance alone. It becomes response. "Come to Me, all who labor and are heavy laden, and I will give you rest" (Matthew 11:28). The call answered is to step into life shaped by Christ rather than just merely surviving.

Testimonies like this matter because they give permission to admit that staying too long can happen to people of faith and that God's presence was not absent even when clarity came late. Scripture assures us, "If I make my bed in the depths, you are there" (Psalm 139:8). Scripture sustains what experience alone cannot explain.

May this book meet you where you are and remind you that survival was/is never the end of your story.

Prophetess Silvonya Powell

ACKNOWLEDGMENTS

First, I thank God.

Not for easy answers or quick resolution, but for presence. For staying when I could not carry everything anymore. For truth that did not rush me, and grace that did not require performance.

This season revealed who and what could remain. Many people could not. Some relationships fell away quietly. Others ended abruptly. What remained was smaller, but it was real.

To my daughters—thank you for your patience, your honesty, and your love during a season when I was learning how to listen more carefully, both to God and to myself.

AUTHOR'S NOTE

This book was written slowly.

Not because the story was unclear, but because it required patience—both from me and from the truth it carries. Much of what appears in these pages unfolded over years and was understood only in retrospect, sometimes long after it happened.

This is not a book about blame. It is a book about patterns—how they form, how they persist, and how they quietly shape a woman's sense of safety, faith, and self.

For years, while awake, I carried a recurring image of myself as a woman cracked from head to toe—broken but still standing. The image appeared repeatedly and without invitation. It did not change. It was how I saw myself.

While some details have been altered to protect privacy, the integrity of the experience remains unchanged.

If you are reading this while carrying your own questions, your own fatigue, or your own history of endurance, you are welcome here. You do not need to agree with every conclusion or share every belief to recognize the posture this story describes. This book does not ask you to rush. It asks you to notice.

Read at your own pace. Pause when you need to. Trust what rises in you as you do.

—Dr. Melba

EPIGRAPH

"Record my misery; list my tears on your scroll—
are they not in your record?"
~ Psalm 56:8 (NIV)

CHAPTER 1
WHEN SURVIVAL BEGINS

There were pictures of me smiling as a baby. One of me dressed exactly like a tall doll I had. Pictures of my brother and me at his birthday party—at home, handing him a dollar and kissing him on the cheek. Pictures of me bundled up in winter clothes, my mother holding me. Pictures of my brother and me standing outside in the snow. Another of us at the beach. A family portrait with my mother, my sister, my brother, my sister's oldest son, and me. And more. Many more family moments captured in Polaroids and others developed from film.

I don't remember any of those moments.

What I do remember was louder than the pictures showed. It was the sting of words. The pain that sat behind the big, beautiful brown eyes staring back at me from those photographs. The sharpness that followed me every day, looming like a ticking time bomb waiting to go off. Loudness transcended generations. Somehow, though, it skipped me.

Arguments didn't belong to just one relationship or one generation. My aunts and uncles argued openly with my mother. My aunts spoke to my grandmother with harsh tongues, and my grandmother absorbed it all in silence, choosing not to respond. My mother kept careful track of how my father's side of the family treated my brother—always making sure he was included—while insisting I stay away. She taught me, directly and indirectly, that only her side of the family wanted to be bothered with me. That distinction mattered. It created a division I learned to live inside.

From little, I understood that I occupied a different place in the family. Not fully claimed. Not fully included. Loved, perhaps—but conditionally. I learned to move through rooms with that awareness, present but careful, close but never central. Being different came with consequences, and staying quiet felt like the safest way to avoid them.

In my family, words like *loca* and *loco* were used casually, offered as explanations for any behavior that didn't make sense or didn't conform. I was used to being asked, "What, are you crazy?" when I did something my mother didn't agree with. The word was normalized. Expected. Desensitized.

I didn't just hear it, I internalized it.

Along with it came the idea she voiced outright: that there was something wrong in my head, some kind of bad blood that needed to be beaten out. Those were her words.

Maybe that was why.

Maybe that was why I didn't belong the way others did. Why silence became necessary. Why staying small felt safer than being seen. Being different was not celebrated. It was corrected.

Silence became adaptation.

Invisibility became survival.

By the time I was old enough to understand the adult tensions and unspoken loyalties shaping our lives, instability had already been normalized. Chaos was not an interruption. It was the background. A constant.

Speaking often came with consequences. When I spoke, I was told to stop. To be quiet. In Spanish, the word cállate can mean either be quiet or shut up, depending on tone and context. I was told cállate all the time. Unfortunately, it wasn't the gentle version. I was being told to shut up—and the way it was said made that unmistakably clear.

But silence didn't protect me either. Even when I chose not to speak, I was in trouble for saying nothing. I would get whoopings for not answering, and whoopings for not saying what was wanted to be heard. There was no safe response—only punishment.

My grandmother later said she believed my stuttering came from being silenced so often, from not being allowed to speak freely. I stuttered badly in Spanish for years. Words caught in my throat. Sentences came out broken. Eventually, I grew out of it—but the habit of holding things in did not leave so easily.

I also learned to keep my feelings to myself. Feelings were attached to words, and words were getting me in trouble. Besides, no one seemed to want to deal with them. The people who were supposed to care did not ask what I thought or how I felt, or they were too busy talking about what they were sacrificing to raise me—how no one else was around to help.

To this day, my mother still says, "*yo me rejodí,*" when she talks about raising us.

Not *jodí.*

Rejodí.

The word matters.

In Spanish, *jodí* means I messed up my life. I screwed myself over.

Rejodí raises the level. It means I did it again. I made it worse. I screwed my life up again—*because of this*. Because of raising you.

She says it as explanation. As justification. As something final.

The message is not subtle.

Raising us did not just cost her something—it ruined her again. It compounded the damage. It marked her life as something permanently diminished by motherhood.

That message didn't feel metaphorical. It felt literal. It taught me that my existence was not just a burden, but a repeated loss. That I was not simply difficult or inconvenient—I was the reason her life never recovered.

I was made to feel like a bother. A burden. A nuisance.

And the fact that she still says it—to this day—taught me that silence was safer than defense, and invisibility was safer than presence.

Silence didn't erase the need to speak; it just pushed it somewhere safer. What I couldn't say out loud had to go somewhere, and eventually it found its way onto paper.

Writing didn't interrupt anyone. It didn't provoke correction or punishment. It didn't require permission. On the page, words could exist without consequences. They could stay as long as I needed them to.

When I was in junior high, I wrote a short story called *Rebuilding My Life*. When the contest was announced, I was excited to enter. Once I started writing, the story took on a life of its own. I did not yet have language for why I was writing it—only the need to do so.

The story centered on starting over, on rebuilding something damaged, on believing that patience and endurance could restore what had been broken. I remember being aware, even then, that the words came easily—almost too easily. I worried that the school might think I was experiencing abuse to that degree, which I was not.

Did I understand some level of it? Yes. Maybe that was why the words flowed the way they did.

When I was in junior high, I wrote a short story called *Rebuilding My Life*. That story appears in full in the appendix, exactly as it was written.

It won at the school level and then at the city level, and my picture appeared in the local newspaper. Adults praised my talent. My mother stood beside me, smiling, even though she could not read what I had written because of the language barrier. I accepted the praise politely from those who offered it, but with a kind of distance, not knowing how to receive it. I did not yet understand that my voice was forming—or that writing was doing for me what it did for Daniella.

It reflected what I already believed: that if you stayed long enough, tried hard enough, waited faithfully enough, things could be made right.

I talked to God during those years, but not in formal prayers. I didn't have the language for that yet. I talked to Him the way you talk when no one else is listening. Sometimes I wrote to Him. Sometimes I just spoke quietly, inside my own head. It wasn't doctrine or ritual. It was conversation. It was a place to put my thoughts when there was nowhere else to put them.

It was escape, too.

I learned how to imagine long before I knew how to hope. I didn't have dreams I could remember from those years, but I had wishes. I wished for better. I wished for something different than what surrounded me. I watched television shows where families were kind to one another. They argued, but they still loved. They disagreed, but no one disappeared. No one was shamed for speaking. Those shows became places I could go when my own world felt too loud.

I had imaginary friends. An imaginary boyfriend who treated me right—not in a grown way, not with romance or expectation, just with kindness. Someone who listened. Someone who showed up. Someone who didn't make me feel like a burden for existing. Those imagined relationships were a way out. A way to step into a version of life where care was steady and I was safe.

At school, I watched other kids my age laugh easily with their friends. I noticed who felt comfortable, who belonged, who moved through the world without bracing themselves. I wondered what their lives were like when they went home. I wondered how it felt to be happy without trying so hard.

I will never forget the first time I went to a friend's house to play. Her mother asked if I wanted to stay for lunch. I agreed. I was shocked when her father, mother, and my friend all sat down together at the table—with a place set for me.

The meal was simple: a sandwich with chips and a drink, and apple pie for dessert. I still remember it. Her parents talked casually, making conversation as they ate. No one was angry. No one was rushing. No one was correcting anyone.

My friend ate her food quickly and told me to hurry up so we could go back outside before I finished. I guess I ate too slowly. I was too busy taking it all in.

That was the day reality met imagination.

Eventually, I needed somewhere to go—not just somewhere to imagine.

As soon as I was old enough to leave the house by myself, my escape became the library. I could take the bus downtown and disappear for hours at a time. I could sit in a library all day, finishing entire books, disappearing into stories where problems had arcs and endings, where people were explained, where resolution was possible.

Books became my refuge long before I understood the word *refuge*. Reading gave me order when life did not.

In books, there was logic. There were beginnings and middles and ends. There were reasons for why people acted the way they did. There were consequences that made sense. I stayed inside those worlds as long as I could because they asked nothing of me except attention.

I did not come into this story looking for language. I wasn't searching for words or meaning, I already lived inside two of them. Spanish and English. I am bilingual. My mother used to say it was like being two people in one.

But in our house, only one of those people was allowed to exist.

English was not welcome at home. We would get in trouble for speaking it. Only Spanish. What was supposed to be a gift felt more like a test—one I was never quite sure how to pass.

Spanish, in my house, carried strain. It carried correction. It carried rules about who I was supposed to be. I was told I was too "Americanized," that I had been raised to be a "Dominican." Whatever that meant. Don't say this. Don't say that. Speak this way. Not that way.

Language wasn't just how we communicated. It was how I was measured, corrected, and found lacking. Carrying more than I could name—even with two languages—I learned early how exhausting it was to constantly monitor who I was allowed to be. I was tired in ways that sleep does not fix, aware even then that something inside me had reached its limit.

All of this happened before I had language for relationships, roles, or futures—before life began asking anything of me out loud.

Before I ever entered a long-term relationship, before motherhood, before vows, before storms, before unraveling, a girl was becoming a woman—shaped quietly by endurance, responsibility, and survival. That shaping was dramatic, layered with loss, harm, confusion, and survival that would take years to untangle.

I needed to escape the noise. The chaos. I needed an exit. I could not do it anymore. I needed an out. If not now, then when?

When the first real door opened, I walked through it.

CHAPTER 2
LEARNING TO WAIT

Leaving did not feel like freedom at first.

It felt like exposure.

When that girl, now turned woman, stepped forward into her own freedom, she carried with her everything she had learned to survive.

I stepped into adulthood carrying survival instincts that had kept me alive but had never been questioned. I knew how to endure. I knew how to adjust. I knew how to stay. These skills had protected me for years, but they had never been examined. I did not yet know how to discern what was actually safe from what was simply familiar.

Leaving was my choice.

But waiting came with me.

I wanted my own place. I started looking at apartments quietly, knowing I needed to leave from under my mother's control. I also knew I did not want to remain in the same religion anymore, which had already become a point of contention between us. That decision alone carried weight I did not yet know how to name.

When my aunt—on my father's side, the same side my mother insisted did not want anything to do with me—heard what I was planning, she stepped in. She invited me to visit my uncle in Miami. It was meant to be a pause. A chance to get away. Space to think.

I had already graduated from high school. I wasn't going to college. Not yet. The hope was that I would like it there, that distance might open something up, that maybe I would decide to enroll once I saw what else was possible.

I took them up on the offer and went to visit.

The rest was history. But history doesn't erase patterns. It just gives them new scenery.

Miami offered movement—noise, color, possibility—but it also demanded discernment I had not yet developed. Freedom came quickly. Wisdom did not. I was young, eager to belong, and determined not to return to the life I had left behind. Independence felt intoxicating. I made choices that felt like agency but were still shaped by scarcity and fear of loss.

I was single in Miami.

I dated here and there. I went out occasionally. But what became clear quickly was that sex functioned as currency there. It was assumed. Expected. Transactional. You went out one time, and by the end of the night, the assumption was that sex would follow.

That wasn't my world.

I wasn't putting out. And that refusal came with consequences I hadn't anticipated. One man left me stranded after a date, saying he needed to grab something from his car and never came back. I stood there waiting until I finally had to call a friend to come get me. Another man offered to buy rims for my car if I slept with him. Others made their expectations clear without ever asking what I wanted.

Once, while I was standing at a bus stop, a man trying to pick me up rear-ended the car in front of him.

It was ridiculous.

Friends back home warned me. They told me Miami was promiscuous. They told me to come back before I got caught up in something that wasn't me. But by then, I was already sold—not on the culture, but on the independence. On the movement. On the fact that I had left. I stayed.

By the time I understood that other people moved through the world differently—more freely, more boldly—I had already learned to pause. To hesitate. To stay still long enough for permission to arrive. Waiting became a posture I practiced without being asked, something that felt responsible, mature, even virtuous.

I watched first.

Always—before speaking, before acting, before deciding where I belonged.

I watched adults argue and then act as if nothing had happened. I watched affection appear and disappear without warning. I watched people leave and return on their own terms. From an early age, I learned that timing mattered—and that the safest timing was rarely mine.

I learned to wait for moods to pass. For voices to soften. For rooms to feel safe again. That posture followed me into independence. I had learned to be quiet. I had been told to stay out of the way, to listen more than I spoke, to make myself small.

So, when attention came—when I was noticed, pursued, chosen—it felt like affirmation. Being chosen felt like value.

I mistook interest for intention and access for care. I confused availability with commitment. Some lessons were learned gently. Others were learned the hard way. I saw warning signs and explained them away. I told myself I was strong enough to handle complexity, mature enough to manage contradictions. When people showed me who they were, I wanted to believe they would become something else.

Hope lived inside that waiting.

So did belief in potential—in who people might become, in what time might change, in what patience might unlock.

I believed patience could soften what love alone could not. I believed that if my mother had given more patience to me—to us—things might have been different, that she might have been gentler, more loving. I believed that if my father had shown more patience toward her, the potential of our family might have had room to grow.

It wasn't the kind of hope that expects resolution. It was quieter. Thinner.

A belief that endurance would eventually be rewarded—that patience would make me more deserving of what I lacked. I believed that if I could just hold on—stay agreeable, stay faithful, stay flexible—my turn would come.

Over time, that hope stopped living only inside me. It began looking outward—for somewhere, and eventually someone, to rest.

Before I ever saw him, I had already heard about him. I knew of him through someone else—through stories of disappearing acts, missed calls, and confusion that never quite resolved. I remember thinking it was strange, and also thinking it wasn't my business. At the time, confusion still felt familiar. Familiar things rarely raised alarms.

The night I met him, I went to a club with my roommate and a few other people. I wasn't drinking much. I had to take my aunt to the airport early the next morning, and I knew I needed to stay clear. He started talking to me, and I remember pausing long enough to ask my roommate if I should even engage. She told me it was up to me.

I gave him my number and told him he wasn't going to remember it. He said he would. He didn't write it down. He was intoxicated. He asked if I wanted to go to breakfast. I said no—I had to take my aunt to the airport.

The next day, he called.

I was surprised he remembered my number. Later, I would think back on that moment and wish I had left my phone off the hook.

We started seeing each other, and not long after, I found out he was also seeing someone else. What followed was confusion—him unable to decide, explanations that circled without landing, reassurances that never quite became truth. We were on and off. I pulled away. I started seeing someone else. Then somehow, I found myself back with him again.

That became the rhythm.

Eventually, I stopped seeing other people altogether. I stayed by myself. I got into church. I gave my life to Christ. I was working at the church and focusing on being steady, on being grounded, on becoming someone who didn't chase confusion.

When I had my oldest daughter at twenty-two, everything shifted. And when she turned one and I found myself a single mother, I stopped engaging with him completely. I didn't chase him. I didn't look for him. If he didn't check for us, I didn't check for him.

I didn't believe in the idea that having a child together meant you were destined to stay connected. I believed in doing what was right for my daughter, even if that meant separation.

Years passed.

When it was time to plan my oldest daughter's eighth birthday party, he offered to help. That was how we started talking again—through logistics, through coordination, through doing something practical for our child. From there, things slowly rekindled. Not dramatically. Not all at once. Just enough to reopen what I had once closed.

A year later, I had our second daughter.

By then, his son had moved in with us, and I was helping raise him as well. We were all in a two-bedroom apartment, and I made sure we moved into a three-bedroom apartment so everyone could be situated. From the outside, it looked like stability.

But the cheating never stopped.

Even as the household expanded, the instability remained. I was managing children, schedules, space, and responsibility—holding structure together while trust continued to erode.

Marriage entered the picture not as a beginning, but as a solution.

I believed in potential. I believed that once everything slowed down—once we were married, once things were formalized, once there was structure—the whirlwind would settle.

There was no proposal. We bought rings together. We got married in the backyard because everyone was already there. Our children were present, watching something take shape that felt more like a decision than a beginning.

At the time, I didn't see that as a warning. I saw it as adaptability. Marriage did not interrupt the pattern. It absorbed it.

I waited for marriage to steady what had always felt in motion. I waited for responsibility to mature into reliability. I waited for permanence to create safety. Waiting still felt virtuous.

I became skilled at holding things together while pretending I wasn't holding them alone. I managed the household. I smoothed over disruptions. I absorbed disappointment quietly. Silence still did its work.

Marriage hadn't taught me how to stop waiting.

It revealed how deeply waiting was already ingrained.

I didn't yet understand that patience, when it asks you to disappear, is not a virtue. I didn't yet understand that staying can be a skill learned in survival, not a sign of health.

I only knew how to hold on.

And so, I waited. Waiting for clarity. Waiting for change. Waiting for the whirlwind to slow. At that point in my life, waiting was still the language I knew best.

CHAPTER 3
OBEDIENCE AS PROTECTION

By then, I already knew how to wait. Obedience was what I used to justify it.

Obedience entered my life disguised as safety.

By the time I recognized it, obedience had already become a reflex. It was not something I questioned; it was something I practiced. Following rules felt stabilizing. Submitting to expectations felt like structure. Obedience promised order in a world that had rarely offered it.

I had learned early that compliance could reduce conflict. If I did what was expected—if I stayed agreeable, quiet, faithful—things might remain calm. Obedience felt like insurance against chaos. After a childhood shaped by unpredictability, I was willing to pay that premium.

Obedience was rewarded.

I was praised for being responsible. For being mature. For not causing trouble. I learned how to read what people wanted and become it quickly. I learned how to adapt without asking whether adaptation was costing me something. Approval followed obedience, and approval felt like protection.

Faith reinforced that lesson.

I was taught that submission was virtuous, that sacrifice was holy, that endurance honored God. I learned to spiritualize discomfort instead of interrogating it. If something hurt, it meant I was being refined. If something felt wrong, it meant I needed to pray harder, wait longer, soften further. Obedience became not just practical—but sacred.

So, when love required endurance, I complied.

At the beginning, I believed in the idea of building something lasting. I believed effort mattered. I believed patience could correct what time exposed. When problems surfaced, I leaned into endurance, not discernment. I told myself commitment meant staying through uncertainty. That loyalty required tolerance. That leaving would mean failing at something I had already invested too much in to abandon.

I did not arrive at doubt suddenly.

It formed slowly—through repetition, through fatigue, through the quiet erosion of certainty.

At first, nothing felt dramatic enough to name. There were no scenes. No accusations. Just a growing sense that I was working harder to explain things than to understand them. I noticed how often I adjusted my expectations before voicing them, how frequently I softened questions before asking them, how quickly I apologized for reactions I hadn't yet expressed.

When tension surfaced, the explanation was always my tone.

He said I talked to him "any kind of way." That phrase stayed with me. It reframed the conversation before it began. Whatever the issue was—finances, absence, inconsistency—it became secondary to how I sounded when I raised it. I learned to audit myself constantly: my voice, my timing, my phrasing. I wondered if frustration invalidated the concern itself.

I told myself this was maturity. That restraint was growth. That not reacting was wisdom.

I was carrying everything. Bills. Household responsibility. Emotional labor. I was the one making sure things functioned, making sure our lives didn't collapse under the weight of what he would not carry. And yet, when I reached my limit, the story became about my impatience, my sharpness, my lack of grace.

So, I adjusted again.

Self-doubt crept in quietly. I questioned whether I expected too much. Whether partnership was an unrealistic standard. Whether wanting consistency meant I was controlling. I reminded myself that everyone has flaws. That marriage requires endurance. That love means choosing patience over impulse.

I learned how to talk myself down.

Maybe he's tired. Maybe work is stressful. Maybe I'm projecting. Maybe this is what marriage looks like.

Those explanations didn't need to last forever. They only needed to hold long enough to preserve stability. I didn't need certainty; I needed continuity. And continuity, I believed, was proof of faithfulness.

There were absences that were explained away. Stories that didn't quite line up. Trips that felt unnecessary. Calls taken in quiet corners. Moments when intuition stirred but was quickly dismissed.

I talked myself down often.

He wouldn't do this. He wouldn't ruin a good thing. I needed those words to be true. Obedience taught me how to override myself. We saw several therapists.

At first, it was his sister who suggested someone. She was already seeing her, so it felt safe enough—familiar, even. We went together. The therapist listened to both of us, and then she asked him to step out of the room. When the door closed, the air shifted.

She didn't speak carefully. She didn't hedge.

She told me I needed to leave him. She told me plainly that I needed to start coming in on my own—to get my life together, to get myself together. There was no drama in her voice, no urgency. Just certainty.

I didn't know what to do with that kind of clarity.

I told him what she said. I thought honesty was required. I thought transparency was obedience. He was angry. And somewhere beneath the noise of that moment, I remember thinking that God had not told me to leave him—so I wasn't going to. If obedience had kept me safe this long, surely it would guide me now.

Time passed. Problems continued. Situations repeated themselves.

I thought maybe we just needed the right counselor.

This time, I looked for a man. I wondered if he would hear things differently if they came from someone he might respect more. We went once. When we got home, he said he didn't need anyone telling him what to do. We never went back.

Later, when things in my own family life began to unravel, I went by myself. I needed somewhere to speak without managing the room. That counselor suggested I bring him in—said there were things a husband needed to understand, things he needed to support me in. He came once. That didn't last either. Anyone who challenged him, even gently, became someone he refused to return to.

The pattern was quiet but consistent.

I kept going for a little while. Then I stopped.

Church faded too. Survival took over. There was always something more immediate to manage, something that needed to be handled before I could sit still long enough to be helped.

By then, we were living in our house. My days were full before they even began. I rushed home from work so my oldest daughter could take my car to her job. I helped my youngest with homework, cooked dinner, drove her to cheerleading practice, kept the house running. I carried the weight of what needed to be done and told myself this was just what responsibility looked like.

When his stepfather's health declined, we made a decision together. I would continue holding things down at home so he could go be present there. It made sense. It felt fair.

But he didn't go. Not really. Tomorrow became tomorrow again and again. And when his family began to say we needed to do better by them, they didn't see what had already been decided—or what I was already carrying. I was exhausted, still trying to finish school, just beginning my doctoral journey, stretching myself thin in ways no one acknowledged.

The comments came anyway. That not everyone is meant to have a doctorate. That it didn't really matter.

He brushed it off. Said none of that mattered. Said all that mattered was what was happening in our household.

I believed him.

I believed that being on the same page was enough—even when I was the only one holding the book. He continued going out. Continued doing what he wanted. And I continued keeping everything standing.

Even in therapy, I had been explaining. Clarifying. Making things make sense. Protecting the story from sounding worse than it was. I didn't yet know how to hear the pattern for what it was.

Obedience had followed me into every room. Infidelity rarely announces itself. It relies on confusion.

What hurt most was not just what was happening, but how long it took me to stop trusting my own reality. I noticed changes in my body before I consciously acknowledged them. I pulled away physically—not out of anger, but instinct. Something in me knew before I was ready to admit it.

Still, I stayed.

There came a point when the adjustments stopped being small.

I had already learned how to manage discomfort quietly, how to absorb what hurt and keep moving. But over time, the fixes required more effort, more sacrifice, and more rearranging of my life. Each solution had to be bigger than the last to cover what was no longer contained.

I had seen people settle before.

I had watched lives come together on the surface—new jobs, new homes, fresh starts that seemed to soften what had once felt sharp. From the outside, things often looked calmer than they had before. More orderly. More contained.

Maybe Georgia could work for us.

If we changed our environment, maybe the pressure would ease. If we started somewhere new, maybe the distance would quiet what proximity had not. The decision didn't feel reckless. It felt measured. Intentional. Like something people did when they were serious about making things last.

Everything always looks one way on the surface.

I didn't yet know how much could live underneath.

I told myself that sometimes you have to make drastic changes to protect what matters.

But the truth was, I was no longer tending a small injury. I was trying to hold something together that would not close. Each new effort stretched me thinner, asked more of me, required more coverage. And still, what needed attention underneath continued to grow.

Eventually, there was no fix large enough to hide what was happening.

I didn't yet have language for that.

I only knew that I was running out of ways to make things feel contained.

There is a particular kind of fracture that occurs when you love someone who will not tell you the truth. It does not just break trust—it breaks your relationship with yourself. You begin to second-guess your instincts, soften your boundaries, and shrink your expectations until survival feels like success.

Others saw it before I did. Some asked directly why I stayed. Others made comments that sounded like concern but felt like judgment. A few people knew more than they admitted. And I was left holding a truth I was not yet ready to face.

I had been taught to honor marriage without being taught how to recognize when it had already been dishonored.

So, I endured. I rationalized. I waited.

Waiting did not repair what honesty refused to confront.

The fracture widened—not because I lacked strength, but because strength was being used to hold something together that was already coming apart. Obedience protected me from conflict, but it did not protect me from harm.

I did not yet know how to leave. I only knew how to survive.

And survival, when mistaken for love, can keep you trapped far longer than fear ever could.

CHAPTER 4
WARNINGS IN THE NIGHT

The first warning didn't feel like danger. It felt like interruption.

By then, usefulness had already become my role. I was managing, fixing, carrying. I knew how to hold things together even when they no longer made sense. Endurance had trained me to normalize unease and keep moving.

The warnings accumulated.

They came as questions I kept answering for myself. As unease I could not name. As moments I filed away because there was always something more urgent demanding attention.

One night, the warning woke me.

It was late—late enough that the house had already settled, the air heavy with the stillness that comes after exhaustion. I had gone to bed expecting rest. When the phone rang, the sound cut through the quiet sharply, pulling me awake faster than thought.

I checked the time twice before answering.

Calls at that hour were rare. Unexpected. My body reacted before my mind could frame a reason. I sat up too quickly, my heart already racing, a tightness forming in my chest that felt disproportionate to the moment.

When I answered, the voice on the other end was calm.

Not rushed. Not surprised. Measured in a way that felt rehearsed.

There was a pause before he spoke, long enough to register. I listened carefully, aware of how quiet it was on his end of the line. Too quiet. The kind of quiet that suggests someone is being careful.

He mentioned a hotel.

The word landed without explanation, without context that made sense to me. I asked questions the way I had learned to ask them—carefully, without accusation, without urgency. Where are you staying again? Why is it so quiet there? My tone was neutral. My body was not.

My stomach tightened. My hands began to shake, not dramatically, but enough that I noticed. I tried to slow my breathing, reminding myself that fatigue amplifies everything. That grief distorts perception. That the hour itself makes ordinary things feel ominous.

The answers came slowly. Briefly. With irritation that felt out of proportion to my questions.

I did not argue. I did not press.

The call ended without clarity. Without confrontation. Without anything I could point to and say, this is it. I lay back down and stared at the ceiling, unable to sleep. The room felt altered, as if something unseen had entered and refused to leave.

I tried to pray. The words would not come.

My body stayed alert, listening for something else, even though I couldn't have said what that was. I told myself this was not the moment. That rest would restore perspective. That tomorrow would demand steadiness.

Warnings don't always announce themselves. Sometimes they simply wake you up. The warnings continued in daylight.

He said he was traveling for work. I tried to believe him. But the stories thinned. Phone calls came back from places that were too quiet. Calls were taken only after he stepped away. Silence appeared where there should have been background noise.

One night, while I was volunteering at an event, he called me back. The quiet on the other end of the line stopped me cold. I recognized it immediately—the same quiet I had heard years earlier when he used to cheat and would find corners to call me from.

My body reacted before my mind caught up.

Something isn't right.

I asked questions the way I had learned to ask them—carefully, without accusation. Where are you staying again? Why is it so quiet? He sounded defensive, irritated that I would even ask.

After we hung up, I called a friend. I called my daughter. Then I called the hotel he claimed he was staying at.

They had no record of him. Not under his name. Not under the company name. Not under the coworker whose name I found online.

When I confronted him, the explanations shifted. Now it was booked under something else. Now he might work overtime. Now he was coming home. None of it aligned.

And still, I tried to reason my way out of what my intuition already knew. I kept telling myself, This man is not crazy. He wouldn't ruin this. I was talking myself off the ledge of clarity.

Atlanta came during preparation.

There was no margin for disruption. Guests were arriving. Schedules were tightening. Final details demanded attention, and I moved through them with precision, keeping everything intact while quietly registering what was missing.

He was not there.

He said he was in Tallahassee at a tailgate—that a well-known pregame show was happening and everything was chaotic. He said his phone was left in the car. That it was loud. That he had been drinking. That was why he missed my calls.

I did not argue with him.

Not because I believed him—but because I did not have time to engage the lie.

I was not going to let him ruin my daughter's wedding.

That decision came first. Everything else was secondary. I kept moving—answering questions, managing details, entertaining guests, holding the moment steady. I did not chase explanations. I did not press for clarity. I postponed it deliberately.

He did not arrive in Atlanta until the day before the wedding.

He was late to the rehearsal. And so late to the rehearsal dinner that he missed the entire dinner portion. I adjusted again—redirecting attention, smoothing over absence, keeping the focus where it belonged.

At the time, I did not confront what I already suspected.

I contained it.

I told myself there would be space later—after the wedding, after the pressure eased—to deal with whatever this was. In Atlanta, my job was not to resolve the truth.

It was to protect the moment. This was not confusion. It was control.

This was also the time I started going to my doctor more often. Not because I was falling apart. Not because anything dramatic had happened. Just routine visits. Every visit started the same way.

"How are you feeling?"

"I'm fine."

The depression screener kept coming back high. The lab work showed stress. One visit, the smile broke.

“I’m not fine.”

“I know,” he said. “I’ve been waiting for you to say it.”

It was the first time I started taking medication for depression. I went back to my life. But something inside me stopped pretending. The warnings came at night.

I dreamed I was walking. There were two people ahead of me. Familiar enough not to question. A dog moved easily beside us. I was eating from a white styrofoam container as I walked. Nothing felt rushed. To one side was a hill, covered in grass and smooth brown stones. Trees in muted fall colors lined it. People walked and laughed on the hill. It looked normal.

Then I noticed the snakes. Copperheads, large and unmistakable, lying among the rocks. No one else noticed them. One person ran up the hill laughing. Another followed. Don’t they see that snake? One moved.

I said quietly, “I’m not going that way.” I stayed on the sidewalk. The sidewalk was green, steady, and uniform. I walked far enough to consider turning back. But I had gone too far. The sidewalk ended at a black metal fence.

Beyond that it was a steep cement drop. People slid down, unable to stop themselves.

I stayed.

A woman said, “There’s a way across. But not down. Hold the gate. Walk the edge.” I set the container down. The fork stuck out. I scooted back up slowly, aware of the drop. I followed the ledge. I woke while still moving.

There were other dreams.

Driving dreams. We rode together until a fork in the road. Then he was gone. I was alone when it was time to decide.

There were nights in bed when I felt a weight settle beside me. Nights when I tried to say Jesus but couldn't until it finally broke free.

Sometimes he was there. And instead of comfort, he shoved me. Told me to stop. Said I was talking in my sleep again. I was a nuisance again.

That was familiar.

I had been trained to keep going. Keep mothering. Keep working. Keep providing. Keep quiet.

I didn't have language yet.

But I wasn't asleep.

And once that happens, nothing ever returns to how it was.

CHAPTER 5
WHEN SURVIVAL ENDS

Survival did not end because I learned something new.

It ended because I reached the limit of what I was willing—and able—to carry.

By late summer, the truth no longer needed my attention to exist. I postponed engagement with it not because I was confused, but because I was containing it. I knew enough. I was managing around it. Facebook was already telling me more than I wanted to know. Survival had become strategic. I was no longer asking whether something was wrong. I was arranging my life to function despite it.

He began going out of town more.

Trips he took alone—Vegas, a class reunion. Absences that came with explanations that were brief and final, as if questions themselves were unnecessary. I learned to keep the household running while he came and went.

Around that same time, the carpet was ruined.

The dog had destroyed it while confined. I handled it. I arranged the repair. I paid for it. Like so many other things, I absorbed the disruption quietly and kept moving.

We still took family trips.

A week-long cruise in November—without him. Photos posted. Smiles documented. Life continuing in parallel.

What happened next came the day my youngest and I returned from that cruise.

We got home late. The house was quiet. He wasn't there.

I was in the bedroom when I heard a buzzing sound. At first, I couldn't place it. Then I realized it was coming from the man cave. A phone was ringing—from his recliner.

I walked in and found it tucked into the console of the couch. His work phone. The screen lit up with her name.

I answered.

Woman to woman, why do you keep calling my husband?

She sighed. Loudly. She didn't say anything. And she didn't hang up.

I muted the phone, changed my clothes, told my daughter I'd be back, and left.

I drove to the two places I thought he might be. I even paid the cover charge to get into one of them.

When I was leaving the second place, he called my cell phone. By then, she had hung up.

I told him it would have been nice to come home and find him there. He said he thought we wouldn't be back until the next morning since our flight came in late. I said I had stopped by a friend's place but was heading home. He said he had gone out with a friend and was on his way too.

I beat him home.

I put the phone back exactly where I had found it and was already in bed when he walked upstairs.

When he came into the room, I said calmly that she had called. I told him I tried to find him because I figured it was important. I suggested he should probably call her back.

I didn't raise my voice. I didn't flinch.

He stood there with his mouth open.

Then he went into the man cave. I heard whispered tones. When he came back, he said it was a mistake. She had called by accident.

Yeah, right.

Christmas came next. We hosted it. His family traveled to Georgia. Some stayed in our home. I cooked, prepared, opened our space while everything underneath me was already strained.

Before we ate, we stood in a circle holding hands, ready to pray. I ended up directly across from him—not intentionally, just how the circle formed.

And the man of the house cried.

I watched the tears fall, trying to understand what they meant. Was it remorse? Was it grief—missing his mother, hating that she never got to see him living in such a large, beautiful house? Was it pride?

I searched his face for clarity. I thought the moment would reach him. It never came.

Even after Christmas, the absences continued. More trips. More silence. More space I learned to live inside. At the same time, I was planning a wedding.

My birthday came in March. He took me on a trip and paid for everything—the travel, the concert, the gambling money. I had a great time. I really did. We saw Johnny Gill, one of my favorites. We visited Motown. We laughed. We enjoyed ourselves. That's when I said something I did have language for.

I told him I didn't need grand gestures.

The trip was generous, and I appreciated it. But what I needed was help where our life actually lived. My love language is acts of kindness—showing up in the everyday weight. Help with the carpet. Help with the repairs. Help easing the financial strain I was carrying alone.

He heard that as ingratitude.

What I was trying to say was that a weekend away didn't fix what I was coming home to. What he took from it was that what he had done wasn't enough. And at the same time, we were already floating just above water.

By then, I knew he had been unfaithful. And the debt had become unmanageable. I had taken out a second mortgage, thinking it was a good idea. It wasn't. I was robbing Peter to pay Paul, then stealing it back from Paul to give it to Peter so I could rob it again. I sank deeper every month.

Any time I went to him for help, the response was always the same.

"I don't know."

"I don't know what you want me to tell you."

"Let me think about it."

"I don't know what you want me to do."

Sometimes it got worse.

"That's a you problem."

"I never told you to do that."

I cosigned for a truck for him. I bought our daughter a car. When I asked for help paying for it, he said he never told me to buy her that car.

Every time I had money, it went into the house. Into the family.

I decided to sell the house.

After weeks of arguing, we agreed to sell, pay down as much debt as possible, and move into an apartment.

The house was sold in May.

That's how we ended up in the third-floor apartment.

He went to see it. He FaceTimed me from inside. And I cosigned on it.

Eventually, I stopped trying to get answers from him.

What I did next wasn't empowerment.

It was my last attempt at maybe he'll actually want me again.

I had my fupa removed—the part of my body that remained after carrying two daughters with him. Now I'm left with a scar. Not just physical.

Then my grandmother died. When I asked him if he would help me pay to send flowers, he told me he didn't have any money.

Not long after, Jojo died.

Then came the wedding in Atlanta. Surrounded by vows and witnesses, something in me hardened. Decision. I didn't announce it. I didn't explain it. I simply knew I am leaving.

In October, my father died.

The Ledger of Loss

Loss had already taught me how to show up.

When his father died, I was there. When his nephew died. When his ex-fiancé died. When his brother died. When his stepfather died. When his niece died. When his mother died.

Every funeral. Every season of grief, I rearranged my life to hold him.

When it was my turn, the response was different. When my grandmother died, there were no flowers. When Jojo died, there was no space for that grief. When my father died—the man he once told, "Don't worry about Melba, I've got her"—there was no presence. No help. Just a text saying he was praying.

At the time, I accepted it as limitation. Later, I understood it as choice. By November, I moved out. I paid for movers. I paid to start over.

My youngest began having panic attacks—often in the mornings. I couldn't leave for work until she was stable. I took her to the ER multiple times. Eventually, I allowed her to quit her job because she couldn't hold herself together.

The apartment was chaos.

The people upstairs smoked weed constantly. They made noise all night. People walked the stairs at all hours. Our peace was constantly interrupted. I argued with neighbors, demanded quiet, tried to create safety where none existed.

All of this while navigating my own crushed spirit.

The strain followed me to work.

I arrived late. I left early. I missed time because of ER visits, the car accident, and my own mental health deteriorating under the weight of everything. What I was living through was interpreted as incompetence. The context didn't matter. The impact did.

I attempted to file bankruptcy. The paperwork stalled. I am still waiting. What surprised me was not devastation. It was relief. Not emotional relief—somatic relief. My body could finally exhale.

Not long after, I had a dream.

I was sitting on the ledge of a roof. The building had burned, but the foundation was still intact. When he asked what I was waiting for, I stood up and walked through the door lit in yellow.

Survival didn't end in one moment. It ended because the system that required me to disappear in order to function collapsed under its own weight.

Leaving wasn't dramatic. It was necessary. And there was no way back into the life that required me to disappear in order to survive. And leaving was the only faithful thing left to do.

CHAPTER 6
CHRONOS AND KAIROS

Freedom can change your address and still leave your appetite unchanged.

Leaving did not end the cycle.

After everything that had happened, I made the best out of the difficult situation of being in the apartment alone with my daughter. The living arrangements were miserable, but we did the best we could. We were unhappy there, but we survived it.

I went out a few times with friends. I went to a couple of parties. I spent time at a friend's house. It felt good to get out of the apartment and be around people again.

But one night, I did something familiar.

It opened the same door I had opened years earlier—the door that had always led back to him. I don't know how else to explain it except that it felt familiar, and it had been a while. That familiarity led me back to the third-floor apartment again.

We talked. I cried. He apologized. He said he thought I would hate him. He said he came clean about everything. I cried more. I was about to leave, and then it shifted.

What should have ended didn't. It became occasional sneaking over—middle of the night, here and there. It became funny. It became exciting because I was sneaking. I told myself I was in control. I told myself this wasn't the same thing.

One night, while it was actively snowing, my car started sliding through an intersection that was already known for accidents even without bad weather. As I was slipping and sliding, I thought to myself, What in the world are you doing? Why are you out here in the snow? What if you end up in an accident? This makes no sense. You need to get your life together.

That was when I admitted to myself how strong the tie still was.

Even though things were messy, deep down I felt like I was winning something because I had gotten him back. I don't know what kind of logic that was, but when you're in a broken space, it makes sense at the time. That thinking carried it forward longer than it should have.

Eventually, I told him where I lived. He realized how close I had moved. I let him come by. He played with the dog. He spent time with his youngest daughter, who was standoffish at first.

After three months in that apartment, I found another place to live. This time, he helped with the move. I hired movers, but there were things I needed help with. He came and loaded my truck. Later, he helped unload it and put things into the new place.

That's when I said it would have to be real. No more funny business. We would start dating. He would go to church with me. We would start counseling with the pastors. That's what we started doing.

Every Sunday, he met our daughter and me at church. After church, we came back to my place. We had Sunday dinner. We played cards or games. We watched a movie. That became the routine.

We made it to one counseling session with my pastors. I had questions—questions about her, about how things had been possible for them—but those questions were never answered. What mattered was that we only made it to one session.

Then his close friend's father died.

He called to tell me he was going to Florida for the wake, memorial service, and funeral. It was a three-day event. That poured salt on an already open wound. Just weeks earlier, I had gone to Florida to support a close friend whose mother had died, and I went and came back the same day.

While he was gone, something settled. I thought about how he showed up for others. I thought about how he had not shown up for my grandmother. I thought about how he had not shown up for my father. I stopped really talking to him while he was gone. He sent messages asking if I was giving up on him. He said he still loved me. He said he always would.

But I knew. This was never going to stop. Same cycle. Different day.

Around that time, my sleep changed.

I started having dreams where I was walking behind him, calling after him. The sidewalk beneath me would turn translucent, and underneath it were snakes. I kept calling. He kept going.

There were other nights when we were in bed and I woke from nightmares. He would shake me abruptly—no comfort, no reassurance—just shaking me and saying I was talking in my sleep again.

Even asleep, my body was not at rest.

That's when I knew I couldn't do it anymore. The cycle had to end. I had to put myself first. It was time to file for divorce.

With the first attorney I retained, he advised me to put the bankruptcy on hold. Rightfully so, he wanted my husband to be responsible for half of the debt, because he helped incur it. As soon as my husband was served, he lawyered up immediately.

When our youngest daughter turned eighteen, I planned a Caribbean trip for her. The month before she turned eighteen, he stopped providing any type of support. He stopped cold. Even before that, he had only been giving a fraction of what he should have been giving.

At that point, I was disgusted.

I told my attorney to forget it. I needed that money to take care of my daughter anyway, so I needed whatever was left from the retainer. I went to the courthouse myself and filed on my own. I waived child support, even though I knew that under Georgia law I could receive support until my daughter graduated from high school.

At that point, things weren't going well with my job. I was eventually terminated and was only working part time. Things were not stable. But I had to put my faith in God.

While working one of my longest shifts at that part-time job, church was on in the background. The girls were at the house listening to music, watching television, and moving around. I was texting my daughter back and forth because she was at home watching the service. We didn't really like the way the guest speaker was delivering the message. We preferred the senior pastor's style.

It was background noise.

And then something he said caught my attention. Time. Chronos and Kairos. Measured time and interrupted time.

He talked about Moses and the question God asked him: What is in your hand?

The question stopped me. I wasn't emotional. I wasn't inspired. I was interrupted. I couldn't unhear it. What was in my hand wasn't abstract. It was my story. My survival.

Everything I had lived through. Unresolved. Unorganized. But present.

What became clear did not bring relief.

Nothing changed immediately. The legal process continued. Money was still uncertain. Work was still unstable. My daughter still needed more from me than I knew how to give. Life did not slow to accommodate clarity.

What changed was my posture.

I could no longer tell myself I was confused. I could no longer believe I was waiting on instruction. What had been named could not be unnamed, and what I was carrying could no longer be managed quietly.

The systems that had held me together—routine, endurance, faithfulness through silence—were no longer sufficient. I was still moving through my days, still showing up, but there was no buffer left between effort and consequence.

I was exposed.

Chronos continued.

Kairos had spoken.

And everything that had been held together by survival was now vulnerable to collapse.

CHAPTER 7
AT THE FOOT OF THE CROSS

Everything collapsed at once. My job. My marriage. My sense of stability.

I found myself asking God why—not because I believed I was being punished, but because I wondered if I had made the wrong choice coming here. If this move had cost my daughter her safety. If it had destroyed my marriage.

And then I saw it.

I saw myself kneeling at the foot of the cross. Not reaching. Not striving. Just clinging. Safe. Covered. Seen.

That was the best place to be.

That position required nothing from me.

I did not have to explain myself. I did not have to justify the choices I had made or defend the ones I hadn't. My body had finally stopped bracing for impact. The tension I had been carrying in my shoulders and chest loosened, not all at once, but enough for me to breathe again.

Time felt suspended there. Not rushed forward, not pulled backward. Just held. I was aware of how tired I was—tired in a way sleep does not fix. Tired in my bones. Tired of holding things together.

And still, I was held. I was not defeated. I was surrendered.

Faith shifted in that moment. It did not demand answers. It did not rush resolution. It waited for instruction. I stopped trying to fix what had already fallen apart and trusted God to order what remained.

Nothing was in my way anymore.

There was no resistance left to push through. No argument left to win. No justification left to defend. I was no longer negotiating outcomes. I was listening.

At the foot of the cross, I was not invisible. I was not forgotten. I was not late. I was exactly where I needed to be.

CHAPTER 8
ANSWERING THE CALL

Answering the call did not feel heroic. It felt deliberate.

Survival had kept me alive. It could not make me whole.

I had survived silence. Waiting. Obedience. Usefulness. Staying.

Each of those postures had served me once. Each had protected me when I did not yet know how to leave. But they could not carry me forward. What had sustained me was now constraining me.

Resilience had carried me my entire life. God had activated it again and again. But resilience was no longer about bouncing back. It was about standing still long enough to be sent.

Healing did not erase my competence. It reshaped it.

By the time I said yes, I was no longer interested in proving faith. I had learned what unchecked endurance costs, and I was unwilling to offer my life again without discernment.

When I was finally discharged, I sat in my car before turning the key. I did not start the engine. I just sat there—phone back in my hands—breathing for the first time without being observed.

That was when I saw the message.

I had not seen it when it was sent. I could not have. They had taken my phone.

It was from my youngest daughter.

She did not know what was happening. All she knew was that I had gone to the hospital. She did not know about the confusion, the restraint, or the way my words had been misunderstood. She did not know that a husband I was divorcing—a man who had stopped acting as a husband years earlier, if he ever truly had—still had influence over decisions being made about my body and my freedom.

She did not ask questions. She did not demand explanations.

Hey Mommy, I just wanted to tell you that I love you so much. I'm praying that you get better and that you take all the time you need to heal. Please know that I'm here for you no matter what. You don't ever have to lie or hide anything from me. I'll always be by your side, even when you feel alone. You're not alone, Mom. I love you, and I'm so proud of you for getting the help you need. "So do not fear, for I am with you; do not be dismayed, for I am your God. I will strengthen you and help you; I will uphold you with my righteous right hand."

Just remember that God has such an amazing plan for your life. When things get hard, remember He does things for a reason. We go through things for a reason, and He gives His hardest battles to His strongest soldiers.

I cried right there in the car. Not quietly. Not carefully. I cried because while systems debated me, my daughter believed me. I cried because love reached me without interrogation. I cried because someone saw me clearly when so much around me felt distorted.

I had been trying to return to the partial hospitalization program where I already had care and structure—explaining that taking safety precautions did not mean I intended harm. I was not trying to disappear. I was trying to live responsibly. That distinction mattered to me, even when it was missed. What I was told instead was that I could not leave. A nurse made it her business to tell me why.

She told me that one of the main reasons I was not being discharged was because my husband agreed that I needed to be transferred to another treatment facility. I was not told how he had been notified—whether through emergency contact information or another channel—but his agreement was treated as decisive.

I watched another woman be released that same day because her husband agreed to take responsibility for her care.

I was not afforded that option.

In that moment, something hardened—not in bitterness, but in clarity. I understood that as long as a legal tie remained, my agency could still be overridden. Decisions about my body, my movement, my care could still be made without me.

That would never happen again.

Not long after, unemployed and newly terminated from my full-time job, I walked myself to the courthouse. I filed for divorce without an attorney. I waived child support. I walked away from what I was legally entitled to—not because I lacked understanding, but because I had it.

I chose severance over security. Autonomy over entitlement. Freedom over financial leverage tied to his business.

People might think that choice was irrational. It wasn't. It was precise.

I wanted no remaining channel through which decisions could be made about me without me. No lingering authority. No residual control.

I stepped out on faith.

I had no full-time job. I had a part-time position and uncertainty ahead. But I believed God would provide—and so far, He has. Every bill has been paid. Every need has been met.

Provision did not come with excess.

It came with sufficiency.

And that was enough.

In the quiet that followed, one thing became clear. I knew where my joy was. I knew where my peace lived. It was with the Lord.

After everything I had been brought through—every loss, every unraveling, every moment that should have broken me—I could not accept that survival was the conclusion. God had carried me through too much for there not to be something on the other side of it.

There had to be purpose beyond endurance. There had to be meaning beyond survival. I did not yet know what that something was. But I knew this: the only way to find out was to move forward.

I did not have clarity. I did not have stability. I did not have everything together. What I had was a quiet conviction that serving was where I was supposed to be next.

So, I began serving. Not because the pain had eased. Not because things made sense.

I stepped into ministry quietly—taking responsibility without certainty, helping where I was asked, learning as I went, and trusting God more than my capacity.

Not long after, I had a dream.

I was walking with two people who were familiar enough not to question, and a dog moved easily alongside us. I was eating as I walked, holding a white styrofoam to-go container. Walking and eating felt ordinary. Nothing felt rushed.

To one side was a hill, covered in grass and smooth brown stones. Trees dressed in muted fall colors lined it. People walked and laughed there. It looked normal. Familiar.

Then I noticed the snakes.

Copperheads. Large. Unmistakable. Lying among the rocks. Some stretched out completely still. One coiled tightly, heavy and full.

They weren't hiding. They weren't striking. They were just there. What stood out most was not fear. It was that no one else noticed them.

One person ran up the hill laughing. Another followed.

A single thought formed, calm and clear.

Don't they see that snake?

One of the snakes began to move.

I didn't shout.

I didn't try to stop anyone.

I didn't freeze.

I said quietly to myself, I'm not going that way.

I stayed on the sidewalk.

Along the sidewalk, everything was green—steady, uniform. No rocks. No fall colors. Just green stretching ahead of me and behind me.

I walked long enough to consider turning back. The hill would have been shorter. Easier. Everyone else had gone that way.

But I had already gone too far.

The sidewalk ended at a black metal fence. Beyond that it was a steep cement drop. I watched people try to cross it and slide down, unable to stop themselves.

I stayed where I was.

A woman stood nearby and spoke calmly.

There's a way across, she said. But you can't go down that way. Hold onto the gate. Walk the edge.

I set the container down. The fork stuck out.

Then I scooted back up slowly, aware of the drop beside me. I didn't rush. I followed the ledge.

Others followed behind me.

I was still moving—still balancing—when I woke up.

During the holidays, one of my daughters handed me a card. Inside were words describing who she saw me to be—kind, faithful, strong, caring, and joyful. There was artwork too. Roots beneath the surface. The word believe was written clearly.

I held it quietly.

Christ had steadied me, but the hurt was still there. Being held did not mean being healed. It meant I was not alone while the ache worked its way through me.

There was humility in this yes.

Not mastery.

Not arrival.

Availability.

I did not yet know the full cost of sustaining a call.

That lesson would come later.

This chapter is still being written.

I don't know everything yet.

But I am willing.

And that is enough.

CLOSING

If you recognize yourself in these pages—not in the details, but in the patterns—you are not weak, and you are not alone.

This book is for women who stayed.

Women who learned how to survive inside relationships that required them to shrink, explain, endure, or disappear to keep the peace.

It is for women who looked up one day—ten, fifteen, eighteen years later—and realized that survival had quietly become an entire way of living.

If that is you, hear this clearly: staying did not mean you lacked strength.

It meant you were carrying far more than you should have had to carry alone.

Many women leave harmful relationships and rebuild. Others stay far longer than they ever intended, believing patience would soften what honesty never confronted. They build lives, families, and routines until one day they realize they must learn how to live all over again.

If you are in that place now, you are not late.

You are not foolish.

You are not beyond repair.

My faith has been present throughout this story—not as performance, but as anchor. I believe that healing and freedom come through Jesus Christ, not through striving or endurance, but through grace.

If you are curious about faith, unsure what you believe, or simply tired of carrying everything on your own, you do not have to have the right words. You do not have to know how to pray. You do not have to be certain.

Sometimes belief begins quietly.

If, even now, you can acknowledge that Jesus is the Son of God, that He died for your sins, and you invite Him into your life as you are—that is salvation. In that moment, you are saved, and something new begins. You are no longer surviving alone. God enters the story with you, and the work of transformation has already started.

If you want to know God, you can begin exactly where you are. Grace does not require preparation. It meets you in truth.

Rebuilding after long survival takes time. Learning how to listen to yourself again, how to trust your discernment, how to live without bracing—this is slow work.

Keeping God first does not mean staying where you are harmed.

It means choosing truth over confusion, alignment over endurance, life over mere survival.

Some days faith will feel steady. Other days it will feel fragile. Both are part of the journey.

And if you are starting over later than you planned, remember this:

nothing you lived through is wasted.

nothing you survived disqualifies you.

God is a redeemer of time.

"I will restore to you the years that the locust has eaten" (Joel 2:25).

Freedom does not erase the past.

It redeems it.

“And we know that all things work together for good for those who love God, who are called according to His purpose” (Romans 8:28).

REFLECTION & INTEGRATION: RETURNING TO THE STORY

The reflections that follow are intentionally tied to the chapters you have just read.

They are not summaries, and they are not conclusions. They are invitations to return—to notice what stood out, what stirred recognition, and what felt familiar before you had language for it.

You may find yourself wanting to turn back to earlier pages. That is not disruption; it is immersion. Meaning often forms when story and self-meet more than once.

You do not need to answer every question.

You do not need to write anything down unless you want to.

You do not need to arrive at clarity.

If you choose to write, space has been provided.

If you choose not to, that is not avoidance—it may simply be timing.

Move at your own pace.

Reflection — Chapter 1: When Survival Begins

Reflection

- Where did survival begin for you?
- What did you learn early on about staying safe?
- What felt familiar as you read this chapter?

Reflection Space

Reflection — Chapter 2: Learning to Wait

Reflection

- What have you learned to wait for?
- When did waiting begin to feel responsible—or necessary?
- What did you hope time would fix?

Reflection Space

Reflection — Chapter 3: Obedience as Protection

Reflection

- What did obedience protect you from?
- Where did obedience cost you something?
- What questions did you silence in order to stay aligned?

Reflection Space

Reflection

- What warnings did you recognize only later?
- How did your body respond before your mind caught up?
- What did you explain away?

Reflection Space

Reflection — Chapter 5: When Survival Ends

Reflection

- When did survival stop working for you?
- What reached its limit?
- What could no longer be carried?

Reflection Space

Reflection — Chapter 6: Chronos and Kairos

Reflection

- Where were you living by measured time?
- What interrupted that timeline?
- What question are you still holding?

Reflection Space

Reflection — Chapter 7: At the Foot of the Cross

Reflection

- What does surrender look like for you—not in theory, but in practice?
- Where did striving finally stop?
- What felt held rather than fixed?

Reflection Space

Reflection

- What remains after survival?
- What do you already have in your hand?
- What does a quiet yes feel like?

Reflection Space

APPENDIX A

Rebuilding My Life

Selected Excerpts and Reflection from a Junior High Manuscript

Rebuilding My Life was written in junior high and preserved in its original final typewritten form for decades. This appendix contains selected excerpts from that manuscript, followed by a reflective note on their significance.

These materials are not presented to provide a complete narrative account. They are included as witness—evidence of how beliefs about endurance, silence, suffering, and rebuilding were already formed long before adulthood.

The excerpts appear as written, with minor formatting adjustments for readability. Portions of the original manuscript have been intentionally omitted to preserve the scope and tone of Silence & Survival.

Selected Excerpts

Excerpt I — Hidden Survival

Daniella Ramirez is a very bright student with straight A's and attends Jefferson Junior High School. Daniella also has a very big problem, but is very clever at hiding it. How long will she hide her problem—forever? Will she ever decide to get help?

Join Daniella Ramirez in her story of "Rebuilding My Life."

Excerpt II — Endurance as Meaning

What I went through was not a breeze, but very difficult. I had to choose between life and death. Life meant struggling to solve my problems, and death meant throwing the chance for a better life away, suffering along with it.

Why did I choose to live? So, I could suffer more in trying to rebuild my life?

A story kept confidential by many. A story which holds many untold answers to many unanswered questions that many were afraid to ask. A story... my story... which I will tell now.

Excerpt III — Silence and Compliance

It was 8:10 on a Monday morning. I was silently sitting in homeroom, listening to the announcements.

I accepted what the coach had said to me. She only said it with my best interest at heart, and I understood.

Excerpt IV — A Witness Who Saw

"You are the one who struggled and came out on top," said Mrs. Howards. "Remember, if you ever need someone to talk to, I'll always be here."

That was the last time I was at the center as a patient. It was finally time for me to return home.

Excerpt V — The Choice to Stay

"All that is left is for you to give your answer. Are you willing to stay here, as long as it takes, to work for a better life?"

"Yes. I will stay as long as it takes."

Excerpt VI — Rebuilding Defined

From that day on, I struggled to stay alive. I worked toward diminishing what harmed me, little by little.

When I was excused, I knew I had completed the first step toward reaching my goal: rebuilding my life.

Appendix Reflection: Returning to the Story

Rebuilding My Life had to be included in Silence & Survival—not in full, but in witness—because it proves that survival did not begin in adulthood. It began in childhood, before I had language for what I was enduring or tools for how to leave.

I held onto that yellow envelope for decades without understanding why. Through every move—from Rhode Island to Florida, through multiple homes in Florida, from Florida to Georgia, and through multiple homes again—I downsized repeatedly. I let go of furniture, clothes, books, and memories. I downsized from a house twice. I left my husband and moved quickly. Necessity dictated what stayed and what was discarded.

Yet somehow, that envelope survived every purge.

It was not preserved intentionally. I did not frame it. I did not reread it. I did not assign it meaning. It simply remained—untouched, unstained, intact—waiting without my awareness.

What appears in this appendix are selected excerpts from that junior-high manuscript. They are not included for narrative completeness or detail, but for witness—evidence of what was already present before I knew how to name it.

Only later did I understand what my younger self had written.

That story was not creative fiction.

It was early theology.

It was survival theology.

Long before I knew words like endurance, obedience, or discernment, I believed rebuilding required patience, suffering, and waiting. I believed that if you stayed long enough, tried hard enough, endured faithfully enough, restoration would come. That belief shaped my relationships, my marriage, my faith posture, and my tolerance for silence.

The envelope survived because the belief survived.

Every move I made in adulthood mirrored what that story assumed: that rebuilding was something you did quietly, repeatedly, without complaint, and often alone. I was rebuilding my life again and again—geographically, relationally, financially—without realizing I was reenacting a framework I had written as a child.

It was not until I moved with purpose—when survival gave way to awareness—that the meaning revealed itself.

Finding the story at that moment was not coincidence. It was timing that could only be understood in retrospect. The manuscript was preserved until I had eyes to see it—not as nostalgia, but as evidence.

Evidence that God had been speaking before I knew how to listen.

Evidence that my calling did not emerge from chaos, but from continuity.

This book is not just about what happened.

It is about how I learned to stay.

The excerpts preserved in this appendix are the earliest record of that learning.

They are included—not as a full account, but as a witness.

APPENDIX B

Scanned Pages from the Original Final Typewritten Manuscript

The following pages are scanned copies of the original final typewritten manuscript of *Rebuilding My Life*, submitted during junior high school. They are included solely to establish authorship, timing, and continuity. They are not presented for narrative completeness or content review.

[Scanned Page 1 — Original Title and Author Page]

REBUILDING MY LIFE

BY: Melba M. Mota
64 Sterry Street
Pawtucket, RI 02860
(401) 726-0367

[Scanned Page 2 — Opening Framework Page]

2

A little bit about the story....................

Daniella Ramirez is a very bright student with straight A's and attends Jefferson Junior High School. Daniella also has a very big problem, but is very clever at hiding it. How long will she hide her problem, for ever? Will she ever decide to get help? Join Daniella Ramirez in her story of, 'Rebuilding My Life.'

[Scanned Page 16 — Closing Section Reflecting the Decision to Stay]

16

All that is left is for you to give your answer. Are you willing to stay here, as long as it takes, to work for a better life,

I went to group conseling, as well as private counseling. I noticed the length of my stay at the center motioned me to work harder. All of my hard work and determination paid off, for when I was excused from the center, I knew I had completed the first step towards reaching my goal: REBUILDING MY LIFE.

www.ingramcontent.com/pod-product-compliance
Lightning Source LLC
LaVergne TN
LVHW091222150826
845673LV00003B/977

* 9 7 9 8 9 9 1 7 1 9 1 6 2 *